IN GOD
WE TRUST

When
Patriotism
Is Not
Enough

JIM REIMANN
WITH DICK PARKER

ISBN 1-58660-580-1

Cover image © Photonica

The author is represented by Alive Communications Inc., 7680 Goddard St., Suite 200, Colorado Springs, CO 80920.

Published by Promise Press, an imprint of Barbour Publishing, Inc., P.O. Box 719, Uhrichsville, Ohio 44683, www.promisepress.com

Member of the
Evangelical Christian
Publishers Association

Printed in Italy.
5 4 3 2 1

*To followers of Jesus around the world who
desire to leave a lasting spiritual legacy.*

We have been the recipients of the choicest bounties of Heaven; we have been preserved these many years in peace and prosperity; we have grown in numbers, wealth, and power as no other nation has ever grown. But we have forgotten God. We have forgotten the gracious hand which preserved us in peace and multiplied and enriched and strengthened us, and have vainly imagined, in the deceitfulness of our hearts, that all these blessings were produced by some superior wisdom and virtue of our own. Intoxicated with unbroken success, we have become too self-sufficient to feel the necessity of redeeming and preserving grace, too proud to pray to the God that made us.

It behooves us, then, to humble ourselves before the offended Power, to confess our national sins, and to pray for clemency and forgiveness.

—ABRAHAM LINCOLN, MARCH 30, 1863

CONTENTS

Most of us will never know what it feels like to fear being imprisoned for our faith—much less losing our lives. We may never experience the agony of being rejected and isolated for what we believe. But even in the United States we're beginning to see the risks of being "Christian." Last year's terrorist attacks certainly showed each one of us that we live in a very volatile time.

In a practical but very direct way this book calls every believer to walk through the door of opportunity the Lord opened for us on September 11, 2001. Jim Reimann, a member of my congregation, has developed a clear blueprint for living life in what some have called a "new world."

From a spiritual perspective, though, the only things Jim sees as new today are 1) an increased willingness among unbelievers to discuss matters of faith and 2) a renewed urgency for believers to share the gospel while our friends and neighbors are more open than before. Certainly the message of the Cross of Christ remains the same.

Nearly every 9/11 book I have seen has dealt with finding comfort and emotional help in the wake of our great national tragedy. *In God We Trust—When Patriotism Is Not Enough,* however, is much more that that. It's a compelling call to every believer to live in a way that honors the

Lord Jesus Christ and to share the message of His Cross—something we should have been doing all along.

I recommend you read what follows, but be forewarned: This is much more than a book to comfort you—it will challenge you to make every day count as never before!

MICHAEL YOUSSEF, PH.D.
CHURCH OF THE APOSTLES, FOUNDING RECTOR
LEADING THE WAY, PRESIDENT
ATLANTA, GEORGIA

When Truth Leads to Trust

The Setting and Significance of Today's Terror

> *Fear of man will prove to be a snare,*
> *but whoever trusts in the LORD is kept safe.*
>
> —PROVERBS 29:25

> *I say we bomb the hell out of them.*
>
> —UNITED STATES SENATOR ZELL MILLER

APRIL 6, 2000

On a beautiful spring day, I sat on a knee-high stone wall in the shade of the grove of old carob trees between the Dome of the Rock, also known as the Temple Mount, and the El-Aqsa Mosque in Jerusalem. My wife, Pam, and I were leading a tour group to Israel, and we had stopped near the ancient holy site to study the Scriptures with our local guide, Tony. For thirty minutes Tony, a Jewish resident of Tiberias who also keeps an apartment in Jerusalem so he can be a part of the holy city, discussed the history of and his reverence for those few acres around us.

I relaxed and pondered as Tony talked about Abraham and Isaac, David and Solomon, and Jesus Christ, as well as the founder of Islam, the Prophet Muhammad. Tony took great care to speak softly—sometimes almost whispering— especially when discussing the significance of the Dome of the Rock to Jews and Christians. He did not want to risk offending the nearby Palestinians who administer the site (Israeli police remain in charge of security) and who might react violently to his statements.

Then he led us up the stairs and through the archways to the most holy of Jewish land where the Dome of the Rock, an Islamic mosque, now sits. Along the way we talked further about the site's history and significance to Jews, Muslims, and Christians. At the door of the mosque, which was spectacular in its architecture, we told our group that they could go inside for a ten-dollar fee, but that according to the Islamic religious leaders they would first have to remove their shoes out of respect to Allah. Tony, Pam, and I remained outside with many in our group who chose not to humble themselves to a god who was not the one true God.

For several years Pam and I have led tours to Israel, accompanied by Christian authors who serve as teachers and recording artists who perform live concerts. Many hundreds of Americans have gone with us to the various biblical sites across Israel. Each trip leads me closer to the Lord as I walk in His footsteps and as I see Him working in the lives of others experiencing the Holy Land for the first time. When we left Israel for the United States in April 2000, we looked forward to our next visit the following fall, having no idea how different things would be.

SEPTEMBER 28, 2000

The next image I saw of the Temple Mount was on television five months later. On the evening of September 28, 2000, I watched as the heavyset leader of Israel's conservative Likud Party slowly trudged up the ancient limestone stairs of the Temple Mount—the same stairs Tony had led us up in April. Ariel Sharon, the former Israeli war hero, forged ahead, surrounded by a full entourage of government officials and his ever-present security detail, his white hair gleaming in the hot fall sunlight of the arid land. Although the Palestinians controlled this relatively small

11

piece of property, Sharon, with a look of defiance on his face, was determined to demonstrate his sovereign right to visit the holiest of all sites to Jews around the world.

Palestinians saw it differently. They believed that by his presence Sharon, one of the most prominent leaders of Israel who very soon would be elected prime minister once again, was demonstrating Israel's sovereign claims over land the Palestinians controlled, and they immediately rose up in protest. My heart sank as I watched young Palestinian men frantically running across the Temple Mount throwing rocks at lines of Israeli soldiers in full riot gear—helmets, shields, and automatic rifles. The next images I saw were of the area between the Dome of the Rock and the El-Aqsa Mosque. War was breaking out among the trees where Pam, Tony, and I, and our tour group had studied the Scriptures together. These two desperate groups of people, both with deeply held religious convictions and the belief that God was on their side, were violently turning one of the most peaceful spots in all of Israel into a war zone.

Pam joined me, and we watched on television as the relative peace that this land had experienced for several years quickly deteriorated, and we became extremely concerned and dismayed. The very next month we were scheduled to take nearly 425 people there for our next teaching tour. The ministry that I believed God had called me to, and the one that had brought me more fulfillment than anything I had ever done, was in jeopardy.

How could Ariel Sharon's visit to this small disputed piece of land known as the Temple Mount be causing such violent upheaval? And why did he feel compelled to make such a visit—something he must have known would greatly anger the Palestinians? The answer to that question is certainly not a simple one, but over my previous years of visiting the Holy Land and studying its history, the answer slowly took shape and finally became clear in my mind. I had come to realize why this one small area was truly the focal point and spiritual center of the world and thereby a potential hotbed of violence.

So much that has happened in Israel, the West Bank, the Gaza Strip, Afghanistan, Pakistan, New York City, and Washington, D.C., on and since September 11, 2001, has its genesis in that tiny piece of real estate and the people who claim it. Our response to these events must be made with an understanding of the history of the conflict, but more importantly, with an understanding of who God is and what He calls His people to do.

The Temple Mount has a history that dates back to the time of Abraham. It was on this very spot—the site of the Dome of the Rock—that the Jews believe Abraham took his son Isaac to sacrifice him to the Lord. God had said to Abraham, " 'Take your son, your only son Isaac, whom you love, and go to the region of Moriah. Sacrifice him there as a burnt offering on one of the mountains I will tell you about' " (Genesis 22:2).

Years later this site was also the very plot of land King David had purchased as a place of sacrifice once again. The Lord had commanded him through the Prophet Gad, " 'Go up and build an altar to the LORD on the threshing floor of Araunah the Jebusite' " (2 Samuel 24:18). When David obeyed and offered to buy the land from Araunah, the man offered to give it to the king. But David answered, " 'No, I insist on paying you for it. I will not sacrifice to the LORD my God burnt offerings that cost me nothing.' So David bought the threshing floor and the oxen [for the sacrifice] and paid fifty shekels of silver for them" (verse 24).

And it was this holy place of sacrifice that then became the site of Solomon's temple in the holy city of Jerusalem. Around 1000 B.C. Solomon constructed his magnificent temple, a project taking some seven years to complete. It stood until 586 B.C., when the Babylonians destroyed it and took the Jews into captivity. Then, after seventy years of exile, the Children of Israel were allowed to return home and, under the leadership of Zerubbabel and Jeshua, they rebuilt their precious temple. "Then the people of Israel—the priests, the Levites and the rest of the exiles—celebrated the dedication of the house of God with joy" (Ezra 6:16). This city and the site of their temple have remained the focal point of the Jewish people and the land of yearning through their centuries of exile.

I will never forget my initial visit to Jerusalem. As we

approached the city we first stopped at a place called the Promenade, just south of Jerusalem near the town of Bethlehem. From this hill I could see not only Mount Moriah, but also the Mount of Olives, with the Kidron Valley running between the two of them. And although I had never been there before, I had the strangest feeling that I was returning home. Yet for many years I had no burning desire to go to the land of Israel. To be honest, when I left on my first trip there, I wanted to go, but I was still not passionate about it. Today all that has changed. I now go twice a year, and each time I can hardly wait to see Jerusalem once again! In spite of my wonderful experience, I'm sure my feelings are simply a glimmer of what the Jews must have felt upon returning from seventy years of captivity to their homeland. How they must have wept during those years each time they thought of their beautiful city lying in ruins! But, oh, the joy they felt when first glimpsing their holy city once again with their now old and tired eyes!

It was this second temple that was later renovated and enlarged by Herod the Great in the first century B.C. Herod's renovation took forty-six years to complete, as we see in John 2:19–21, which says, "Jesus answered them, 'Destroy this temple, and I will raise it again in three days.' The Jews replied, 'It has taken forty-six years to build this temple, and you are going to raise it in three days?' But the temple he had spoken of was his body."

Over the thirty-three years of His life, Jesus visited the

temple many times, the first when he was only eight days old, and the last shortly before His death. In fact, during the last week of His life, Matthew records the following prophecy Jesus made regarding the destruction of the temple: "Jesus left the temple and was walking away when his disciples came up to him to call his attention to its buildings. 'Do you see all these things?' he asked. 'I tell you the truth, not one stone here will be left on another; every one will be thrown down'" (Matthew 24:1–2). This prophecy was fulfilled in A.D. 70 (approximately forty-one years later) when Titus, the Roman general, moved across Israel in an effort to brutally crush a Jewish revolt against Rome.

On another visit to Israel, Pam and I witnessed evidence of the fulfillment of this prophecy with our own eyes. Standing in a newly excavated site at the southwest corner of the Temple Mount's retaining wall, literally at the street level of Jesus' day, we could see the stones of Herod's temple. Many of them lay smashed at ground level, having been pushed from the higher level of the temple courtyards above. We saw the literal fulfillment of this prophecy, exactly as Jesus had predicted: "Not one stone" was "left on another," having been "thrown down"!

When we consider the history of this place, especially in light of Jewish history, it is no wonder Israel is extremely reluctant to remove its claim to it. In fact, it is much more than a mere reluctance. Even according to Jewish tradition, this summit serves as the center of the world and the foundation of the entire universe. But more than that, the Jews view their claim to Israel, and especially the area of the Temple Mount, as an eternal covenant between themselves and God. How could they ever release their hold on this land when, on the very ground where the Lord changed Abram's name to Abraham, He told him, " 'I will establish my covenant as an everlasting covenant between me and you and your descendants after you for the generations to come, to be your God and the God of your descendants after you. The whole land of Canaan, where you are now an alien, I will give as an everlasting possession to you and your descendants after you; and I will be their God' " (Genesis 17:7–8)!

OCTOBER 30, 2000

The intifada (uprising) that began with Ariel Sharon's visit to the Temple Mount radically changed our business. Within days after September 28, 2000, the number of people scheduled for our tour the very next month dropped dramatically. At one point our group that once numbered nearly 425 seemed to be dwindling almost hourly, and I wondered if the business would survive.

It was a perplexing time. Several years earlier a friend, Marc Ratner, had shared his remarkable calling in life to take people to the land of Israel. And from the very first day of learning of his dreams and aspirations to "make the Bible come alive for people in the Holy Land," I was hooked! It was as though the Lord had given me the same yearning and desire to see lives transformed by visiting the land where Jesus was born, ministered, died, and rose again.

Marc and I could not have been more different from each other, which made our ministry all the more remarkable. God had chosen to put Marc, a Messianic Jew, and me, an evangelical Christian of Austrian-German descent, together to take Christian believers to Israel.

As of September 2001, we had already been involved for several years in taking many hundreds of people to the land of the Bible. Pam and I were the hosts and teachers on the tours, while Marc handled nearly everything behind the scenes. We were a wonderful team, and the tours had quickly become our primary ministry and business.

With cancellations now pouring in after the start of the intifada, with violence in Israel in the daily headlines, and with the U.S. State Department warning Americans not to travel there, we were faced with an extremely difficult decision. Should we take our dwindling group of "diehards" to Israel in spite of the warnings, or should we take what many were calling the "commonsense approach" and stay in America where we were safe? For me the decision was black-and-white, and so-called common sense should not come into play. To me the issue was a spiritual one.

Frankly, I was very disappointed with the tremendous amount of fear that our group of American Christians was expressing. Every day Marc and I were doing a great deal of "hand-holding" with believers who made no effort to hide the sheer terror in their voices. If people decided not to go with us, so be it. But the great amount of panic and fear these people were exhibiting seemed contrary to what the Bible refers to as walking in faith, "For God hath not given us the spirit of fear; but of power, and of love, and of a sound mind" (2 Timothy 1:7 KJV).

Besides, God is sovereign! If He had called us to go, and if He had called these 425 people to sign up to go, didn't He know then that the intifada was going to take place later? For me the answer to that could never be in doubt. Therefore, I felt we must go!

Even from a purely practical standpoint, the decision to go seemed reasonable, although a number of people thought we were crazy, and some even told us so! I reasoned that simply living life anywhere—even in America—carried a certain amount of risk. Riding a tour bus in Israel for ten days seemed much safer to me than driving the busy interstate highways of America's bustling cities during that same time period, and government statistics bear me out on this one. I knew that not one American tourist had been a victim of terror in Israel. God is not just God in America. He is fully capable of protecting us wherever we are in the world.

I do not want to overspiritualize our decision, but quite honestly, I felt like the apostle Paul, who at one point in his ministry was determined to go to Jerusalem in spite of the danger facing him there. Acts 21:12–13 says, "The people. . .pleaded with Paul not to go up to Jerusalem. Then Paul answered, 'Why are you weeping and breaking my heart? I am ready not only to be bound, but also to die in Jerusalem for the name of the Lord Jesus.' " Like Paul, I was determined to go, and this passage became for me a strong confirmation that Pam and I were in the center of God's will.

   With the decision to move ahead decided once and for all, we quickly communicated to the people who had not yet canceled that the tour was still a go. Yet daily the numbers continued to decline. We had a number of prominent Christian authors and musical recording artists scheduled to travel with us, and most of them felt it was "prudent to cancel." Believing God would provide speakers and musicians for our times of praise and worship in Israel, we moved ahead. Besides, one musical group was hanging in there with us—that is, until ten minutes before Pam and I left for the airport! Now we were left to do all the teaching, and there was no one remaining to lead us in songs of worship.

By the time our plane landed in Tel Aviv, Israel, we found our numbers had dropped to eighty-five—a far cry from the original 425. My heart ached for the nearly 340 people who may have missed what could be their only opportunity to visit the Holy Land for a very long time to come. Undeterred by our now much smaller group, we were determined to provide these brave souls the tour of a life-time. And I will never forget what one of our guides told his group as soon as they boarded their tour bus: "Thank you for letting Jesus be your guide, instead of CNN." Like many of us, he knew, at least at that point, that the media was portraying the situation in Israel in a much more desperate light than the reality of the situation warranted. The violence at that point had been contained to places we would never even consider visiting with our tour groups.

We had the tour of a lifetime. Because tourism had already declined so much in Israel, we had many sites completely to ourselves, and by being able to get around more quickly we were able to add at least seven additional sites to our itinerary. Plus, the Lord provided Israeli Christians who were in ministry there to speak to our group and to lead us in praise and worship. As a result this tour became much better than any we had previously experienced.

The most amazing thing about this particular tour was what happened on the final day. We always end the tour in the peaceful setting next to the Garden Tomb in Jeru-salem. Although you would think that the remaining eighty-five of the original 425 people would be courageous "diehards" and all very strong Christians (which is exactly what I had thought), I felt the Lord leading me to give an invitation for some of them to come to a saving knowledge of Jesus. Before we had our communion service, I told the group, "Wouldn't it be a shame to have traveled all this way, to have learned all that we've learned about Jesus, and to have walked where He walked and have seen what He saw, but return home to America without knowing Him?"

To my amazement six of our group of supposed Christians prayed to receive Christ as their personal Savior! For me, no other confirmation would ever be needed to prove that we had made the right decision to operate the tour. Often I have wondered where those six souls would be today if we had stayed home in the so-called safety of America.

Once this tour was over we were forced to face the reality of what greatly reduced numbers would mean to our ministry and business in the future. It seemed obvious that tours with hundreds of people would not materialize for some time to come, yet by watching our expenses very carefully we felt we could hang on to this ministry we dearly loved. After crunching the numbers, we determined that even groups of eighty or so would allow us to hold on financially—at least until some relative peace could be found between the warring parties in Israel.

SEPTEMBER 7, 2001

In early September Marc and I placed all our advertising and printed more than one hundred thousand brochures to advertise tours for 2002—thousands of dollars worth of investment in a ministry I knew was my calling.

I knew when I wrote the checks that peace does not come easily in Israel, especially at the holiest site in Jerusalem. What we know as the Temple Mount is known in Arabic as El-Haram esh-Sharif, or the Noble Sanctuary. This land, which is considered hallowed land to Muslims the world over, now houses two mosques that are vitally important to every follower of Allah and his prophet Muhammad.

The first is the Dome of the Rock Mosque, the third most important Islamic sanctuary in the world. It was built between A.D. 688 and 691, and more than thirteen centuries later, its golden dome remains one of the most exquisite landmarks in all of Jerusalem. In fact, to this day, nearly every television news reporter filing a report from this holy city stands on the Mount of Olives, with the golden Dome of the Rock visible in the background. Surely it is the most recognizable landmark in all of Israel.

The Dome of the Rock Mosque is the most ancient Muslim monument in the Holy Land, having been built over a huge rock that measures fifty-nine by forty-three feet. Islam teaches that it was from this very rock that the prophet Muhammad ascended into heaven. Yet to the Jews, this rock represents something much different. To them, it is the altar upon which Abraham placed his son Isaac, as recorded in Genesis 22, and was later incorporated into the temple or its complex of buildings. The channels that have been chiseled into it indicate that it was indeed used at some point in its history as an altar for regular animal sacrifices.

Just a few hundred yards away at the southernmost point of the Temple Mount stands the El-Aqsa Mosque, the primary place of Islamic worship in the land of Israel. Every Friday, the holy day of the week for Muslims, huge crowds converge at this site for their noon prayers. Yet because the violence of this most recent Palestinian uprising began at this very mosque, and because the government of Israel controls the access to the Temple Mount area, young Palestinian men have been restricted from attending their Friday prayers in an effort to decrease the violence. Of course, many believe this has only contributed to the violence happening elsewhere across Israel.

The El-Aqsa Mosque, like its neighboring mosque, is also quite ancient. Its construction began less than twenty years after the completion of the Dome of the Rock, so it is nearly thirteen hundred years old as well. Together these two mosques represent the first great religious complex in the history of Islam. The choice of this site for two of the most important mosques in Islam was most likely a political issue, however, since Jerusalem is never even mentioned in the Quran. In locating his mosque on the former site of the Jewish temples, the caliph Abd el-Malik meant to reinforce the idea that the new religion of Islam and its worldly empire was not only the continuation of, but also the successor to, the faiths of all Jews and Christians.

In light of the history of this place, literally dating back thousands of years, it is not hard to understand how difficult (if not impossible!) any peace agreement centering on Jerusalem and this holy place can be reached. Any kind of compromise seems unlikely, because the Jews and Palestinians alike believe they have a God-given claim to this same small piece of land.

Not only do the Jews and Palestinians lay claim to the Temple Mount, but many Christians view it as a holy place as well. In some respects, it could even be said that the story of Jesus began there. It was in the temple that Zechariah, the father of John the Baptist who would become the forerunner of the Messiah, was approached by an angel of the Lord, as recorded in this passage from Luke's gospel:

> *Once when Zechariah's division was on duty and he was serving as priest before God, he was chosen by lot, according to the custom of the priesthood, to go into the temple of the Lord and burn incense. . . . Then an angel of the Lord appeared to him, standing at the right side of the altar of incense. When Zechariah saw him, he was startled and was gripped with fear. But the angel said to him: "Do not be afraid, Zechariah; your prayer has been heard. Your wife Elizabeth will bear you a son, and you are to give him the name John. . . . And he will go before the Lord in the spirit and power of*

27

Elijah, to turn the hearts of the fathers to their children and the disobedient to the wisdom of the righteous—to make ready a people prepared for the Lord."

LUKE 1:8–9, 11–13, 17

So with three of the world's largest faiths laying claim in one way or another to this one small plot of land in Israel, it is difficult to paint the future prospects of peace in this troubled land with anything but a dismal brush. With thousands of years of a turbulent history to remember, not to mention the current escalating violence, an agreement that will fully satisfy both Jews and Palestinians alike seems to be increasingly impossible. When it comes to a number of political issues, compromise requiring both sides to soften certain demands may be possible. Even when it comes to negotiating a peace agreement that requires each side to share the land of Israel, compromise may be possible. Yet, in my view, all the negotiations in the world will never be able to settle the issue of who should control the Temple Mount area. How could either side give up what they deem to be theirs in perpetuity?

The Scriptures emphatically tell us that there will never be lasting peace in Israel until Jesus returns. Therefore, when you hear of peace negotiations and possible solutions, remember what the Lord said about Ishmael and his Arab descendants, " 'He will be a wild donkey of a man; his hand will be against everyone and everyone's hand against him, and he will live in hostility toward all his brothers' " (Genesis 16:12).

Surely the reality of these ancient words is being played out every day in the news!

SEPTEMBER 11, 2001

For more than two hours, Marc had tried in vain to phone me. My family and I were on vacation at a beach in the panhandle of Florida, and although I am typically an early riser, I was sound asleep at 10:00 A.M. Central Time. The phone rang, and as I was quickly summoned, the nightmare of 9/11 began for me.

"Is your television on?" Marc questioned, with a tone of panic in his voice.

"No, I slept in this morning," I responded.

"They've flown planes into the World Trade Center! They've collapsed. They're completely gone, and all the people in them. The news says as many as fifty thousand people may be dead!"

"Turn on the TV!" I shouted.

Over the next hour the horrid details of what has become known as "9/11" and "America Under Attack" began to unfold, and for the remaining four days of my vacation, I remained glued to the relentless television news coverage of America's darkest hour since the attack on

Pearl Harbor sixty years before.

In total disbelief—again and again—I watched the videotape of an airplane smashing into the World Trade Center. Each time I saw it my reaction was the same: "This can't be happening!" I knew what this day would come to mean for me and for the ministry I loved.

"Marc, we're out of business," I told my dear friend and partner in ministry. Within a mere matter of minutes the reality of 9/11 brutally slammed into my world and that of Marc's. The so-called safety of America had vanished with it.

We were forced to see our ministry and business being taken from us by Islamic terrorists who flew planes into buildings! Needless to say, it was difficult to understand how this could be in God's plan for us. From an intellectual and spiritual perspective, I knew beyond the shadow of a doubt that the Lord was still in control and seated on His throne. My emotions, however, seemed to be telling me another story altogether!

I know many thousands of people were suffering in much more grievous ways than I as a result of 9/11, and I was indeed thankful that all of my friends and family were safe. Nothing could compare to the loss of life that so many people were experiencing, and even though my loss was not nearly as great, I was experiencing the death of a ministry I dearly loved. What continued to gnaw at me was that it had literally been taken from us by people we would never know, and through no fault of our own. If I had committed some horrible sin and lost the ministry, it would have at least been understandable to some degree.

God had given me many wonderful ministry experiences over the thirty-plus years of my walk with Him, but I could honestly say that nothing I had ever done compared to seeing the transformation that took place in peoples' lives during a visit to Israel. We had seen a number of people come to a saving knowledge of Jesus, even people who had long thought they knew Him, but didn't! We had seen hundreds of people return to the United States with a renewed love of the Savior and a much deeper understanding of His Word.

Now all that had been taken from us in a matter of minutes. What was the message that God had for me in all of this? Was there a purpose in this for me? Was there a message He wanted me to share?

It wouldn't be long before I would have my answer.

SEPTEMBER 16, 2001

Whose promises are you standing on today?

A ten-foot-long American flag hangs in the foyer of our home as a reminder of our love for the United States of America. As I walk under the stars and stripes from my study to the living room, I am reminded of the promise of our country's Declaration of Independence that our government was instituted to secure my God-given rights to "life, liberty, and the pursuit of happiness."

We depend on our president and the military, which for four years included our son Jeremy, who served in the United States Navy on the USS *Enterprise*, to protect the promises we have come to rely upon.

Today, however, we come face-to-face with an enemy who would strip away every bit of life, given the opportunity, a "pestilence that stalks in the darkness," a "plague that destroys at midday" (Psalm 91:6)—and we shudder.

"Our terrorism is a good accepted terrorism because it's against America," Osama bin Laden said on a video-tape following the September 11, 2001, attacks against the United States. In another tape he made reference to "the first martyrs in Islam's battle in this era against the new Christian-Jewish crusade led by the big crusader Bush under the flag of the Cross. . . . We ask Allah to make him [Taliban leader Mullah Mohammed Omar] victorious over the forces of infidels and tyranny and to crush the new Christian-Jewish crusade. . . ."

Sitting in church with my family on September 16, 2001, I knew this was the place this war would be won: in the presence of God. President George W. Bush and our military will not stop the evil that attacks our souls and our spirits without our prayers and God's protection.

After church I asked Pam, our three children, and our two daughters-in-law to gather in the living room of our home. It seemed to be no coincidence that we were all together for the first time in more than two years just five days after September 11.

"The media has characterized this attack as a wake-up call for America," I began, "but I see it as a wake-up call for us as Christians. We are facing a spiritual attack, and as a family of God we must draw a spiritual line in the sand, just as President Bush is drawing a military line in the sand to protect our nation. The years ahead are going to become more and more challenging for us as Christians, and if we are going to leave a spiritual legacy, we must all become more spiritually mature, not riding the spiritual coattails of our parents, but relying on the strength of our own relationships with the Lord. God has only children, no grandchildren, so we are each accountable for our own growth in Him. We must accept all of the responsibilities that come from being children of God. If we are going to prevail in the years ahead and take a strong stand for Him we must spend more time in His Word and in prayer. Your Mom and I have always prayed that 3 John 4 would be true in the life of our family: 'I have no greater joy than to hear that my children are walking in the truth.' But that will not be true if we do not know His truth, and we will not know His truth without spending time each day listening to Him as we read and study His Word and speak to Him through prayer."

This book is a reminder that when patriotism and the

promises of men and nations are not enough, God promises to protect us from pestilence and plague. Yet I believe we must trust Him, acknowledge His name, and call upon Him. Our national motto is, "In God We Trust." The time has come for us to live up to those four words—to stand on His promise, to call upon God daily, to spend time in His presence and His truth, and then to listen to Him speaking to us through His Word, as we sit quietly before Him.

Commit your way to the LORD;
trust in him and he will do this:
He will make your righteousness shine
like the dawn,
the justice of your cause like the noonday sun.
Be still before the LORD
and wait patiently for him;
do not fret when men succeed in their ways,
when they carry out their wicked schemes.
—PSALM 37:5–7

Because I know whom I have believed,
and am convinced that he is able to guard
what I have entrusted to him for that day.
—2 TIMOTHY 1:12

When Light Overcomes Darkness

In him was life,
and that life was the light of men.
The light shines in the darkness,
but the darkness has not understood it.

—JOHN 1:4–5

A day cannot live in infamy without
the nourishment of rage.
Let's have rage.

—*TIME* MAGAZINE,
SPECIAL EDITION, SEPTEMBER 2001

For the first time in a generation, America has seen the face of hatred so intense that it wants only to destroy, and the sight of it chills us to the bone. We have seen the face of evil so hideous that it drives us behind locked doors. So we unfurl our American flags, and we become patriots again, united and indivisible. We sing "God Bless America" with feeling for the first time in decades, and we expect God to "stand beside us and guide us."

Then we go about our business just as before, except for a lingering pang somewhere in the pits of our stomachs as we worry that our guns and our bombs and our missiles might not defeat this enemy.

We have depended for so long on our nuclear warheads to protect us, we have forgotten how to depend upon God. Now comes an enemy that only He can defeat, and we don't even remember how to ask for His help.

This book is a reminder, a refresher course for people who would seek the face of God. But before you read further, understand that God isn't looking for lip service. He's looking for men and women who will stand up for Him, seek His face, and proclaim His Word. He doesn't need crosses on our lapels any more than He needs flags on our cars. He wants our hearts, our minds, and our lives. Then He will use our lives to create a spiritual legacy "to all nations" (Luke 24:47).

If we are ever going to do anything in our spiritual walk, now is the time.

The initial response to the images of the collapsing World Trade Center towers was profound disbelief, shock, and sorrow. For many Americans in the months that followed, those emotions gave way to fear that evil would triumph, and they numbly plodded through their days wondering when the next attack would come. Others chose to follow the lead of United States Senator Zell Miller— "I say we bomb the hell out of them"—and believed *Time* magazine when they read that America needs to "relearn why human nature has equipped us all with a weapon. . . called hatred."

History has shown the fallacy of both fear and hatred.

Dr. Billy Graham, three days after the attacks on New York and the Pentagon, told the nation, "We're facing a new kind of enemy. We're involved in a new kind of warfare, and we need the help of the Spirit of God."

The following Sunday morning, churches all across America were filled to overflowing. Many Christians (and many unbelievers as well) had an innate sense that we need God's help to defeat this evil, and we came together to worship Him, ask for His help, and plead for some sense of perspective in a world suddenly turned on its head.

Yet God will not sanction our fear in this fight; neither will He assist those who return hatred for hatred. God requires something even more daring and bold if we are to defeat this evil: a response laced with courage and love.

Do not misunderstand me; I do not offer these thoughts

as a pacifist. Our nation has been attacked, and our country must continue to respond appropriately. We have an enemy whose declared goal is to kill us and to destroy our nation. When threatened in this way, we have every right to protect ourselves and to remove the threat, even when it means killing the enemy.

But this battle must be waged in two ways to be effective—militarily and spiritually. (I am sure others more qualified than I will discuss the best military methods.) There can be no question that we as Christians should, and must, pray for the protection of our country, our military leaders, and all those in our armed services. We must ask the Lord to grant His wisdom to our president, his cabinet members, and our strategic military planners, knowing that ultimate victory in the battle of good versus evil will occur not on the battlefield, but within the confines of the human heart.

We are not alone. Before Jesus was crucified, He promised God would send "another Comforter, that he may abide with you for ever" (John 14:16 KJV). God fulfilled that promise with the Holy Spirit, who so emboldened the early Christians that they risked their lives in order to proclaim the gospel. Within a few years of the crucifixion of Jesus Christ, the preaching of the apostles through the inspiration of the Holy Spirit led to the conversions of thousands of people—primarily Jews—to Christianity.

It was the evangelistic success of the apostles that led

to their persecution in the first century, and in the twenty-first century, Christians across the world are still being persecuted for evangelizing. Christians in America have, for the most part, been spared threats of violence, but our brothers and sisters in other countries are beaten, imprisoned, and killed every day by repressive governments and individuals who hate the message of Christ and would exterminate all Christians, if given the opportunity.

Samson Olushola of Nigeria is one of many examples. Samson is Nigerian National Director of Ambassadors for Christ International. In January 2000 he was leading a group of seven hundred people toward a river where fifty believers were to be baptized. A mob of Muslim extremists attacked the group, and Samson was beaten until he was unconscious. For some time his doctors did not know whether Samson would survive this vicious attack. Not only did he survive, he is now back baptizing believers he has brought to Christ, and he is continuing to trust God to take care of him.

Would we trust Him so completely?

FIRST-CENTURY TERRORISTS

The first Christian persecutors were Pharisees, a group of fundamentalist Jews. They hated the followers of Christ and Jesus Himself, believing Christ and His followers polluted the purity of Jewish law. Jesus healed people on the

Sabbath, ate with sinners, and touched those deemed unclean. Perhaps worst of all, Jesus taught that God offers salvation as a free gift to anyone, not just those made worthy by adhering strictly to Pharisaic laws. They began killing Christians in the name of God, just as Jesus had predicted: " 'A time is coming when anyone who kills you will think he is offering a service to God' " (John 16:2).

Saul of Tarsus described himself as "a Hebrew of Hebrews" (Philippians 3:5) and said, "According to the strictest sect of our religion, I lived as a Pharisee" (Acts 26:5). As a result of his fanaticism, he became what might be classified today as an anti-Christian terrorist. The Bible says Saul "breath[ed] out murderous threats against the Lord's disciples" (Acts 9:1). He received authority from the high priest to take Christian men or women as prisoners to Jerusalem, where they were tried and imprisoned or stoned. He even engaged spies to identify their own family members as Christians so they could be taken away and stoned.

For several years Saul apparently watched, or perhaps even participated in, this cruel form of public execution where people pummeled the victim with stones until he or she lay bruised and bleeding, and finally died. His heart must have been as black as coal and as cold as stone. Yet he was a proud man—a Jewish lawyer, or Pharisee, who most likely could have recited the Torah (the Old Testament books of law) from memory—and in his hatred for impurity he was convinced his terrifying actions were a service to God.

Saul was so determined to crush the Christian movement he set out on a trek from Jerusalem to Damascus, a difficult journey of about 150 miles. His plan was to arrest any and all Christians and bring them back to be stoned for blasphemy, according to his understanding of the Jewish law.

As Saul made his way toward Damascus to strike terror into the hearts of as many Christians as possible, God shone a light into his cold, dark heart. God used the brightness of His light to strike Saul with blindness. In a vision the Lord told Ananias, a Christian disciple, to go to Saul and restore his sight by placing his hands on him. But Ananias was afraid to go because of Saul's murderous reputation. Then came God's amazing statement to Ananias: " 'Go! This man is my chosen instrument to carry my name before the Gentiles and their kings and before the people of Israel' " (Acts 9:15).

The impossible was happening! God was so dramatically changing Saul's heart that He was about to use him to carry the Gospel message to Jews and Gentiles alike. The Lord took this first-century terrorist and transformed him into the apostle Paul.

As we can see from this account, terrorism is not a phenomenon new to the twenty-first century. In fact, not only was Saul of Tarsus a person who terrorized the early Christians, but later, as the apostle Paul, he was mistaken for an Egyptian terrorist upon his arrest in Jerusalem. The

Roman commander asked, " 'Aren't you the Egyptian who started a revolt and led four thousand terrorists out into the desert some time ago?' " (Acts 21:38). Apparently terrorists were quite common during the first century as well.

Throughout his life, Paul never forgot who he had been, and he often pressed the point that if he could experience a change of heart, any heart could be changed, no matter how dark, no matter how bleak. When God's light shone into that darkness, the darkness could not overcome it.

THE WORLD'S BIGGEST BARNS

Persecution of Christians continued, but now Saul the hunter became Paul the hunted. He and others were beaten, whipped, and jailed. Despite these tactics aimed at frightening first-century Christians, those who received the Holy Spirit continued to preach the message of Christ publicly, and the church grew by the thousands all across the Mediterranean basin.

It was a model of growth that had been repeated many times before among the people of God. Whenever the nation of Israel had experienced good economic times, they believed their blessings were a result of their own actions and turned away from God. When tests came—famine or attack from nearby enemies—they would turn back to God, confess their sins, and thereby experience a renewal of hope.

It is not surprising then that the Christian church,

which finds its root in the Jewish nation—"You. . .have been grafted in among the others and now share in the nourishing sap from the olive root" (Romans 11:17)—has experienced its greatest revivals during times of crisis. Church growth in the United States often follows a crisis such as war or economic depression. In the last half of the twentieth century, however, Americans faced few crises that, in their minds, required the services of God. We have stood on our own and built the world's strongest nation.

Why, then, are we now so quickly thrown into a panic? More specifically, why do Christians who claim a God who promises to stand by us in any circumstance allow our fears to overwhelm us? Is it because we have so much to lose?

I am reminded of the parable Jesus told of the rich man who built bigger barns in which to store what the man called " 'my grain and my goods' " (Luke 12:18). His life was taken from him that very night. In relating the story, Jesus said, " 'This is how it will be with anyone who stores up things for himself but is not rich toward God' " (verse 21).

In our relatively brief history, the United States of America has been blessed like no other nation in history. As with the rich man in the parable, the ground under us has produced a bountiful crop. But with blessings come responsibilities. " 'From everyone who has been given much, much will be demanded; and from the one who has been entrusted with much, much more will be asked' "

41

(Luke 12:48). Historically we have used a portion of our bounty to share the gospel with the world. More recently we have focused increasing attention on building the biggest barns the world has ever seen and filling them to the rafters with "our goods and our grain."

We have placed our trust in our retirement accounts and our real estate, despite Christ's instructions immediately following the parable of the rich fool: " 'Do not worry about your life, what you will eat; or about your body, what you will wear. . . . Who of you by worrying can add a single hour to his life? . . . And do not set your heart on what you will eat or drink; do not worry about it. . . . But seek his kingdom, and these things will be given to you as well' " (Luke 12:22, 25, 29, 31).

Our only hope is in Him. We must follow His battle plan against evil. We must pray not just daily or even hourly for peace. "Pray continually" (1 Thessalonians 5:17) and God will give us peace, although not necessarily an end to external conflict. " 'Peace I leave with you,' " Christ said, " 'my peace I give you. I do not give to you as the world gives. Do not let your hearts be troubled and do not be afraid' " (John 14:27).

He promised us peace in Him! He pointed out this profound contrast when He said, " 'I have told you these things, so that in me you may have peace. In this world you will have trouble. But take heart! I have overcome the world' " (John 16:33).

We who are His followers will overcome the world as well and the evil thrust upon us, but only by fighting the battle as God directs. Are we willing to allow Him to work through us to win the hearts and minds of our enemies?

Though I am free and belong to no man,
I make myself a slave to everyone,
to win as many as possible.

—1 CORINTHIANS 9:19

Pray for us that the message of the Lord
may spread rapidly and be honored,
just as it was with you.
And pray that we may be delivered from
wicked and evil men,
for not everyone has faith.
But the Lord is faithful,
and he will strengthen and protect you
from the evil one.

—2 THESSALONIANS 3:1–3

When Prayer Leads to Peace

Peace I leave with you; my peace I give you.
I do not give to you as the world gives.
Do not let your hearts be troubled
and do not be afraid.

—JOHN 14:27

I'd like to see the world for once
All standing hand in hand
And hear them echo through the hills
"Ah, peace throughout the land."

—THE NEW SEEKERS

I grew up in the Age of Aquarius—the 1960s, when young people across the nation painted peace signs on walls and greeted each other with the casual lifting of two fingers. "Peace, man. Make love, not war."

As the 1970s began, with no end in sight to the Vietnam War, John Lennon gave the Woodstock generation a new motto: "All we are saying is give peace a chance." Then Coca-Cola aired one of the most popular television commercials of all time: "I'd like to teach the world to sing in perfect harmony."

Peace—the world's peace—was a rock 'n' roll festival on a farm in New York or a chorus of people from across the world holding hands on a beautiful hillside and singing about drinking a Coke. Everyone, it seemed, was talking about peace, and yet those years are remembered by most people in my generation as the least peaceful, most turbulent time of the twentieth century.

The peace the world sought could not be achieved. That's not a pessimistic statement. It's plain fact. Even if we could convince nations to lay down their weapons and lock arms in unity, then criminals, inner-city gangs, and extremists would assail us in the pursuit of their own desires.

Many of the peace protesters themselves proved the impossibility of their own kind of peace by spitting in the faces of soldiers returning from Vietnam and throwing stones at "fascist pigs," better known as police officers. These protesters may have had "peace" written on their signs, but they did not have it written on their hearts. The flowers of "the flower power movement" had quickly wilted, and violence took their place.

A RADICAL'S "PEACE"

We called the protesters radicals, but their ideas paled in comparison with the radical nature of the apostle Paul's prescription for true peace: "Do not be anxious about anything, but in everything, by prayer and petition, with thanksgiving, present your requests to God. And the peace of God, which transcends all understanding, will guard your hearts and your minds in Christ Jesus" (Philippians 4:6–7).

This is the peace that I believe every human being on earth seeks—peace in our hearts, minds, and souls. The apostles, in their search for peace, did not ask Christ to teach them to sing in perfect harmony. Instead, they said, "Lord, teach us to pray. . ." (Luke 11:1).

We should begin our search for peace in prayer as well, just as our nation did in another time of great crisis. The Civil War was not going well in the latter half of 1862. In August the outmanned Confederates defeated Union soldiers at the second battle of Bull Run, sending the Union army retreating to Washington. Eighteen days later the Confederates were stopped at Antietam in the bloodiest day in United States military history; twenty-six thousand were dead, wounded, or missing. Then in December, 12,653

Union soldiers were lost in the defeat at Fredericksburg, Virginia.

President Abraham Lincoln, seeking peace in the land, appears to have understood the way to find peace in our hearts as well. In March 1863, he issued a proclamation designating "a day of national humiliation, fasting, and prayer. And I do hereby request all the people to abstain on that day from their ordinary secular pursuits and to unite at their several places of public worship and their respective homes in keeping the day holy to the Lord and devoted to the humble discharge of the religious duties proper to that solemn occasion."

In making his proclamation, President Lincoln's observation of our nation was eerily similar to what we see in America today:

We have been the recipients of the choicest bounties of Heaven; we have been preserved these many years in peace and prosperity; we have grown in numbers, wealth, and power as no other nation has ever grown. But we have forgotten God. We have forgotten the gracious hand which preserved us in peace and multiplied and enriched and strengthened us, and have vainly imagined, in the deceitfulness of our hearts, that all these blessings were produced by some superior wisdom and virtue of our own. Intoxicated with unbroken success, we have become too self-sufficient to feel the necessity of redeeming and preserving grace, too proud to pray to the God that made us.

It behooves us, then, to humble ourselves before the offended Power, to confess our national sins, and to pray for clemency and forgiveness.

When President Lincoln prayed for peace, it wasn't the sweet, hand-holding peace young people would sing about one hundred years later. It was God's peace—a lasting peace in the hearts of all people. It behooves us again today to humble ourselves before God, confess our sins, and pray for clemency and forgiveness—and for peace.

We must pray for the president as our nation's leader and as a professing member of the Church, the body of Christ. " 'Who knows but that you have come to royal position for such a time as this?' " (Esther 4:14). As brothers and sisters in Christ with our president, we pray not only for him, but also alongside him.

Pray that we, and the president, will see this battle with spiritual eyes, as the prophet Elisha did when he was surrounded by the Syrian army. When Elisha's servant saw the army with horses and chariots, he asked in fear, " 'Oh, my lord, what shall we do?' "

" 'Don't be afraid,' the prophet answered. 'Those who are with us are more than those who are with them.' And Elisha prayed, 'O LORD, open his eyes so he may see.' Then the Lord opened the servant's eyes, and he looked and saw the hills full of horses and chariots of fire all around Elisha" (2 Kings 6:15–17).

Through our prayers we must call the heavenly hosts into the fight on our behalf, to pray for their active engagement. For the war against evil will be won, " 'Not by might nor by power, but by my Spirit,' says the LORD Almighty" (Zechariah 4:6).

MODERN PARTICIPANTS IN AN ANCIENT WAR

For centuries, "Ground Zero" in this conflict has been Palestine, and the twenty-first century effects of war on the people of that land are not very much different than those experienced in Old Testament times. A friend whom I met while leading tours has a beautiful gift store in Jericho, located in the West Bank. Israeli troops have closed off the city, so my friend is now out of business. Another friend, a Palestinian Christian, has a store in Bethlehem, also in the West Bank, near the Church of the Nativity. On a typical day in recent years, 150 to 200 tour buses would bring tourists to his neighborhood so they could visit the place said to be the birthplace of Christ. Now there are none. In a country heavily dependant on tourism, thousands are out of business.

This conflict that has reached our shores began thousands of years ago—even before Elisha saw the chariots of fire—and the Bible tells us it will continue until the end of time. " 'Teacher,' they asked, 'when will these things happen?' . . . He [Jesus] replied: . . . 'When you hear of wars and revolutions, do not be frightened. These things must happen first, but the end will not come right away.' Then he said to them: 'Nation will rise against nation, and kingdom against kingdom' " (Luke 21:7–10).

In Jewish, Christian, and Muslim tradition, we hold up Abraham as God's great man of faithfulness. "Abram [later Abraham] believed the LORD, and he credited it to him as righteousness" (Genesis 15:6). But Abraham had his moments of failure. The consequence of one of those failures resounds even today.

The Lord told Abram, " 'Look up at the heavens and count the stars—if indeed you can count them.' " Then he said to him, 'So shall your offspring be' " (Genesis 15:5).

Abram believed the Lord, but his wife, Sarai (later Sarah), who was childless, became impatient. Taking matters into her own hands, she told Abram, " 'Go, sleep with my maidservant; perhaps I can build a family through her' " (Genesis 16:2).

Abram agreed, and the Egyptian maidservant Hagar became pregnant. But this was not the Lord's perfect plan. He told Hagar through an angel, " 'You shall name him Ishmael. . . . He will be a wild donkey of a man; his hand will be against everyone and everyone's hand against him, and he will live in hostility toward all his brothers' " (Genesis 16:11–12). God later promised Hagar, " 'I will make him [Ishmael] into a great nation' " (Genesis 21:18), but this would not negate the previous prophecy that he would "live in hostility toward all his brothers."

Fourteen years later, Abraham and Sarah still did not have a child together. When the Lord said again that Sarah would bear a son— " 'I will make nations of you' " (Genesis 17:6)—Abraham fell on his face and laughed. But God was true to His word. Isaac was born.

Abraham asked God to bless both Ishmael and Isaac. The Lord blessed them both, but He said He would establish His covenant through Isaac, whose offspring became the Hebrew nation. " 'And as for Ishmael. . .I will make him fruitful and will greatly increase his numbers' " (Genesis 17:20). His descendants became the Arab nations, and throughout the centuries the Arabs and Jews have fulfilled the prophecy of Genesis 16:12, living in hostility toward one another.

Satan takes advantage of those hostilities to further his spiritual battle against God's forces of good. He leads extremists to use the message of Islam to inflame hatred for all Jewish people and, by extension, all Christians, for through Christ we have been grafted into the tree of Abraham. The Bible teaches that, as Christians, we are adopted sons and daughters of Abraham. Therefore, we are natural objects of Satan's hatred. The terrorists who would kill every American might not realize or even recognize this, but Satan certainly does.

My pastor, Dr. Michael Youssef, is well acquainted with Islamic thinking. He was born and reared in Egypt and in 1983 wrote in his book *America, Oil, & the Islamic Mind,* "Muslims cannot differentiate between the western way of life and the Judeo-Christian ethical systems. Even though the Judeo-Christian heritage has greatly influenced our standards and values, it is not exclusively identified as the whole. But to Muslims, America is synonymous with Christianity." Later he helps explain why Islamic extremists would target us, by relating, "A temporary gain or loss in income will not slow the majority of the Islamic world in its drive to carry out its mission of chipping away at Christianity, which Muslims perceive to be their number one rival because of Christian missionaries, not only in the West, but also in Africa and parts of Asia." After all, America, over the last two hundred years, has sent more missionaries into the world to spread the gospel than any nation that has ever existed.

In spite of what we have heard recently in the media—that Islam is a religion of peace—Michael Youssef stated in his book, "There are only three alternatives for dealing with non-Muslims under the Islamic legal system: (1) they must be converted; (2) they must be subjugated; or (3) they must be eliminated (except for women, children, and slaves)." Once we begin to understand this, perhaps we will no longer be so surprised that many in the Islamic world would like to destroy us as Americans and as Christians. In fact, to them an American is a Christian, and, therefore deserving of their hatred.

Also, we should not be surprised when a terrorist takes control of an airplane, for Satan is "the prince of the power of the air" (Ephesians 2:2 KJV). He used his domain to attack our country, which has taken its stand for good. "For our struggle is not against flesh and blood, but against the rulers, against the authorities, against the powers of this dark world and against the spiritual forces of evil in the heavenly realms" (Ephesians 6:12).

"PRAYER IS THE BATTLE"

Just as we as Americans have now been warned to "be alert," the apostle Paul warned first-century Christians: "With this in mind, be alert and always keep on praying for all the saints" (Ephesians 6:18).

Paul tells Christians in Rome and in Ephesus to arm themselves through prayer for the fight that quickly approaches: "The hour has come for you to wake up from your slumber. . . . The night is nearly over; the day is almost here. So let us put aside the deeds of darkness and put on the armor of light" (Romans 13:11–12). "Put on the full armor of God so that you can take your stand against the devil's schemes" (Ephesians 6:11).

The armor of God, as Paul describes it, includes:

- The belt of truth buckled around your waist.

- The breastplate of righteousness.
- Feet fitted with readiness that comes from the gospel of peace.
- The shield of faith with which you can extinguish all the flaming arrows of the evil one.
- The helmet of salvation.
- The sword of the Spirit, which is the word of God.

When you have prayed for and received the full armor of God, you are ready to "stand your ground. . .stand firm" in prayer (Ephesians 6:13–14).

Oswald Chambers, in *My Utmost for His Highest,* wrote, "Prayer does not equip us for greater works—prayer is the greater work. . . . Prayer is the battle."

This war will be won on our knees, as God ultimately will bring our enemies to theirs. "Some trust in chariots and some in horses, but we trust in the name of the LORD our God. They are brought to their knees and fall, but we rise up and stand firm" (Psalm 20:7–8). Christ understood that when He prayed for us, as written in John 17:15, " 'My prayer is not that you take them out of the world but that you protect them [meaning us, who are followers of Christ] from the evil one.' "

If I had asked Jesus what to pray for me, I would have said, "Take me out of the world. Don't just protect me. Get me out of here!" But that was not His will for us.

" 'As you sent me into the world, I have sent them into the world,' " He prayed (John 17:18). So He prayed for our protection against evil, and He admonished us, " 'I am sending you out like sheep among wolves. Therefore be as shrewd as snakes and as innocent as doves' " (Matthew 10:16).

Paul also asked his fellow Christians to pray for his protection. When he was going to Jerusalem, he did not know what trouble he would encounter. " 'I only know that in every city the Holy Spirit warns me that prison and hardships are facing me' " (Acts 20:23). So he wrote the Christians in Rome, "I urge you, brothers, by our Lord Jesus Christ and by the love of the Spirit, to join me in my struggle by praying to God for me" (Romans 15:30).

In those prayers he found peace and assurance: "In our hearts we felt the sentence of death. But this happened that we might not rely on ourselves but on God, who raises the dead. He has delivered us from such a deadly peril, and he will deliver us. On him we have set our hope that he will continue to deliver us, as you help us by your prayers. Then many will give thanks on our behalf for the gracious favor granted us in answer to the prayers of many" (2 Corinthians 1:9–11).

God will deliver us into peace as well—"the peace of God, which transcends all understanding" (Philippians 4:7). For Christ is as close to us today as He was to the disciples on the boat when "a great windstorm arose, and the waves beat into the boat, so that it was already filling. But

[Jesus] was in the stern, asleep on a pillow. And they awoke Him and said to Him, 'Teacher, do You not care that we are perishing?' Then He arose and rebuked the wind, and said to the sea, 'Peace, be still!' And the wind ceased and there was a great calm" (Mark 4:37–39 NKJV).

After that marvelous display of His power to calm the greatest storm, Jesus asked the disciples the same question He asks us today:

Why are you so afraid?

—MARK 4:40

When Fear Gives Way to Courage

Jesus took the Twelve aside and told them,
"We are going up to Jerusalem."

—LUKE 18:31

Better a thousand times to die with glory
than live without honor.

—LOUIS VI OF FRANCE

Jesus was walking resolutely toward His death, and He knew it. Yet those closest to Him perceived no fear in Him.

He knew exactly what lay in store for Him in Jerusalem. He would be mocked, insulted, spat upon, flogged, and crucified. Even the disciples understood. " 'But Rabbi,' they said, 'a short while ago the Jews tried to stone you, and yet you are going back there?' " (John 11:8). Jesus could have avoided his fate by simply staying out of the city, but to avoid Jerusalem was to thwart the mission for which He was sent—to redeem you and me. He could not fail. So He walked on, His face set sternly for Jerusalem.

God has likewise laid a mission before each of us individually and as a nation, and if we take up the call, His Word promises that we will endure suffering, sorrow, and pain for His sake. Why would anyone want to go "up to Jerusalem"?

Because He also promises, " 'Never will I leave you; never will I forsake you' " (Hebrews 13:5). He gives us His power not only to endure but also to prevail. He gives us hope—not just the hope we espouse when we say blithely, "Hope you have a good day!"

"We have this hope as an anchor for the soul, firm and secure. It enters the inner sanctuary behind the curtain, where Jesus, who went before us, has entered on our behalf" (Hebrews 6:19–20).

Our hope is anchored by a heavy chain to the very throne of God! It is unshakable and unbreakable because we have an advocate at the right hand of God, Jesus Christ Himself, interceding for us, as though He were saying, "I've paid the price for them. Their hope is based not on what they do but on what I did at the Cross."

With that kind of hope we can endure any and every trial, seeing them as being God's way of conforming us to the image of His Son. The apostle Paul wrote, "Our hope for you is firm, because we know that just as you share in our sufferings, so also you share in our comfort" (2 Corinthians 1:7).

Paul understood these great truths of God when he set out for Jerusalem, despite his friends' warnings: "Through the Spirit [the disciples] urged Paul not to go on to Jerusalem" (Acts 21:4). Then "a prophet named Agabus. . . took Paul's belt, tied his own hands and feet with it and said, 'The Holy Spirit says, "In this way the Jews of Jerusalem will bind the owner of this belt" ' " (Acts 21:10–11). Hearing that, the disciples again pleaded with Paul not to go. But the apostle replied, " 'Why are you weeping and breaking my heart? I am ready not only to be bound, but also to die in Jerusalem for the name of the Lord Jesus' " (Acts 21:13).

Paul was saying, in essence, "So what if I get hurt or even killed? I will go wherever God leads me, and He will take care of me." Paul wasn't being trivial about human life; rather, he saw himself under the shadow of the Almighty, protected as an ambassador of Christ. In God's sovereign plan, it didn't matter if Paul died in Jerusalem or Rome or at sea; he would be protected into eternity.

God will give us the same courage He gave Paul, if we will only trust Him.

"Even though I walk through the valley of the shadow of death, I will fear no evil, for you are with me; your rod and your staff, they comfort me" (Psalm 23:4). Good will triumph over evil only when God is called into the battle, and God fights wars differently than the Pentagon. Take the experience of Gideon, the weakest man in the weakest clan of the weakest tribe of Israel. The Midianites had overtaken Israel, and the Lord turned to Gideon and said, " 'Go in the strength you have and save Israel out of Midian's hand. . . . I will be with you, and you will strike down all the Midianites together' " (Judges 6:14, 16).

Then, to make sure Israel would not boast about its own strength, the Lord told Gideon to send home thirty-two thousand men, leaving him with only three hundred. Across the Jordan River "the Midianites, the Amalekites and all the other eastern peoples had settled in the valley, thick as locusts. Their camels could no more be counted than the sand on the seashore" (Judges 7:12).

Following the Lord's instructions, Gideon had the men go out in the middle of the night and blow trumpets, smash jars, raise torches, and shout, " 'A sword for the LORD and for Gideon' " (Judges 7:20). Their foes fled in fear, giving the battle to the Israelites.

Gideon trusted God, he acted on that trust, and God was true to His word. Jesus said, " 'If anyone chooses to do God's will, he will find out whether my teaching comes from God or whether I speak on my own' " (John 7:17). In other words, we must first step out in faith, choosing to do His will and to believe His word, and then He will march out to battle with us.

Paul said nearly two thousand years ago that we were living in the last days, meaning that time was short. It certainly follows then that we are now two thousand years closer to the end of time today. Or, to put it more personally, I have fifty-two fewer years to take my stand for God and to share His gospel than I did the day I was born. Am I going to wait until I get my household and my finances perfectly in order first? Or wait until my children are grown, out of college, and settled in their careers? Or wait until I have retired? Or will I make today count by sharing the gospel?

And what is the gospel? The apostle Paul said, "I do not fill my sermons with profound words and high sounding ideas, for fear of diluting the mighty power there is in the simple message of the cross of Christ" (1 Corinthians 1:17, TLB).

That simple message of the cross of Christ answers the difficult questions: What are we going to rely on to empower us? Who are we going to trust when it's not easy to take a stand? When everything is thrown at us, do we tuck our tails and run? Do we let someone else take a stand because the cost for us may be too great? The battle has been brought to us, and we must make a decision. " 'Choose for yourselves this day whom you will serve' " (Joshua 24:15).

It's not enough to name the name of Christ and say, "I'm okay because I know Him." We must serve Him and submit to His instructions, which are simple: " 'Go ye into all the world, and preach the gospel' " (Mark 16:15 KJV).

We've been told to share, but how many of us really do? How many of us have the courage to share the truth of the gospel in love?

The first time I visited the Yad Vashem Memorial to the holocaust in Jerusalem, I lasted only fifteen minutes before I broke down and cried. Growing up, I had always been interested in World War II. I had read a lot about the concentration camps and what had been done to the Jews. But walking through Yad Vashem, I saw shoes, eyeglasses, and other personal effects. I saw identification tags for real people who were now gone, and I knew they represented millions of others. The weight of that inhumanity became personal for me for the first time. They were people like me who loved their families, went to work, and one day were taken away and murdered. The thought overwhelmed me.

My wife, Pam, and I host two "Streams in the Desert Tours of Israel" each year, and our visit to Yad Vashem comes on the last day of our tour. From there we go directly to the garden tomb, where Christ's body is said to have been laid. We experience man's depravity in the morning, immediately followed by the greatest act of love ever displayed.

Each time we go to Yad Vashem I am reminded of Oskar Schindler, for the Israelis have planted a tree for him along the Avenue of the Righteous leading to the museum and have inscribed a plaque with his name. Schindler was a German businessman who single-handedly saved eleven hundred Jews from Nazi extermination by posing as a Nazi and then "buying" Jews from the Germans to work in his factory. Schindler is buried in Jerusalem, and I have visited his grave, placing a small stone there in his memory, as is the custom, for flowers fade.

In the final scenes of Steven Spielberg's movie *Schindler's List*, when the Jews have been liberated, many of the people Schindler saved had their teeth pulled and the gold removed from fillings to make a ring for him as a token of their gratitude. On the ring was carved this inscription from the Talmud: "Whoever saves one life, saves the world entire."

Schindler slid the ring onto his finger, but he did not smile. Instead, he pondered what else he might have done, and he said, "I could have got more. I could have got more!"

"But eleven hundred are alive because of you," they said to him.

"I could have done more," he said. "I could have done more. I threw away so much money." Then he pointed to his car and said, "Why did I keep that car? Ten people right there."

Touching the gold Nazi pin on his lapel, he said, "This is gold. Two more people it would have given me. At least one. One more person."

Then he covered his face with his hands in shame. "I could have got one more person, and I didn't," he said through his tears.

Recalling the scene as I stood near the entrance of the empty tomb outside Jerusalem, I confessed to my fellow travelers, "I wonder how many opportunities I have squandered. How much money I have wasted that could have been used for the Lord; all the things I could have done for Him and didn't; all the people who might have been saved!

"Oskar Schindler committed himself to saving the physical lives of Jewish people. God has called me, and you, and all Christians, to spread His word so He can save the eternal, spiritual lives of all people."

Schindler's tears were not unlike those of the shepherd in Christ's parable who had one hundred sheep, and one wandered away. " 'Will he not leave the ninety-nine on the hills and go to look for the one that wandered off? And if he finds it, I tell you the truth, he is happier about that one sheep than about the ninety-nine that did not wander off. In the same way your Father in heaven is not willing that any of these little ones should be lost' " (Matthew 18:12–14).

Schindler saved eleven hundred Jews from certain death but wept over the one lost that he might have saved had he sold his gold pin. I watched him, and I wondered how often we as Christians weep for the lost. How often do we weep for the prodigal, lost somewhere in the city, longing to come home but ashamed of his sins? Jesus said, " 'I tell you, there is rejoicing in the presence of the angels of God over one sinner who repents' " (Luke 15:10).

The Pentagon will never win the war we fight against evil. Only God will. And His weapons are courageous Christians who are willing to march into enemy territory to proclaim the message He gives us. "We are therefore Christ's ambassadors, as though God were making his appeal through us" (2 Corinthians 5:20). An ambassador goes and takes the king's message to the people and to other nations. He can't stay at home beside his warm fireplace and keep that message to himself. If you think you don't have the courage to go out as an ambassador and offer Christ to others, go anyway. He will strengthen you! That He has promised. That is what He demands of us.

The ministry He has entrusted to us is reconciliation, for Paul wrote: "All this is from God, who reconciled us to himself through Christ and gave us the ministry of reconciliation: that God was reconciling the world to himself in Christ, not counting men's sins against them" (2 Corinthians 5:18–19). And the message we must proclaim is simple and clear: "For I resolved to know nothing while I was with you except Jesus Christ and him crucified" (1 Corinthians 2:2).

Christ came to save the world. All He asks us to do is to tell them. Do it, and He will fill you with the courage to stand. Never say, "But, Lord, you don't understand my situation!" The only "but" the apostle Paul used was this:

But we preach Christ crucified.
—1 CORINTHIANS 1:23

Yet when I preach the gospel,
I cannot boast, for I am compelled to preach.
Woe to me if I do not preach the gospel!
—1 CORINTHIANS 9:16

When Suffering Leads to Glory

We do not lose heart.
Though outwardly we are wasting away,
yet inwardly we are being renewed day by day.
For our light and momentary troubles are
achieving for us an eternal glory
that far outweighs them all.
—2 CORINTHIANS 4:16–17

Faith is believing in advance what
will only seem logical when seen in reverse.
—PHILIP YANCEY

God has not given us a complete answer to the age-old question, "Why did the Lord allow this to happen?" Instead, He guides us to the kind of victory over suffering that the apostle Paul experienced. Having been beaten and imprisoned, Paul wrote to Christ's followers in Rome, "In all these things we are more than conquerors through him who loved us. For I am convinced that neither death nor life, neither angels nor demons, neither the present nor the future, nor any powers, neither height nor depth, nor anything else in all creation, will be able to separate us from the love of God that is in Christ Jesus our Lord" (Romans 8:37–39).

In the face of his suffering, Paul was more than optimistic. He was victorious. We can be, too, if we are willing to suffer hardship—if we are willing to move our own man-made abundance out of the way and receive the fullness of God's love.

God wants us to be victors over our abundance and our suffering. It is up to us to relinquish anything that we allow to come between Him and us. Then, He says, He will work through us to achieve victory over any suffering we endure. Jesus said in the Sermon on the Mount (Matthew 5–7) that those who suffer have a special place in the eyes of God. Then He said, " 'The last will be first, and the first will be last' " (Matthew 20:16). Finally, at the end of His earthly life, He—the One who was in the beginning with God and through whom everything in this universe was made— chose to experience suffering and humiliation firsthand by allowing Himself to be nailed to the Cross. Our suffering pales in comparison, yet He understands.

The question for us now is, "How much are we willing to give up, and then suffer, for God?" Or, as Oswald Chambers puts it in his book *My Utmost for His Highest,* "Have we come to the point where God can withdraw His blessings from us without our trust in Him being affected?" I edited the updated edition of *My Utmost for His Highest,* which was published in 1992. As I worked on it from late 1989 through the spring of 1992, my prayer became, "Lord, please make the truths of this book evident in every aspect of my life." I had read this wonderful devotional for nearly twenty years at that point, but when I read Chambers' question on October 23, 1995, as part of his devotion "Nothing of the Old Life!", I still struggled with it. Would I really trust God if He withdrew His blessings from me?

Throughout the year I had felt as though God were raising the question again and again, and each time I answered, "God, I can't say it's completely true in my life, but I want it to be."

In February our oldest child, Jeremy, joined the Navy. My wife, Pam, and I knew our firstborn might someday be asked to sacrifice his life for his country, and that concerned us, but we gave him our full support and prayed for God's protection over him.

Three months later we sold the Christian Armory, a

bookstore we had owned for twenty years. We had twenty-eight employees who were more like children to us, and every day with them had been a blessing. I immediately missed them terribly.

In late summer our church underwent a terrible split in the congregation, and the upheaval took much of the enjoyment from our times of corporate worship.

Then in September our middle child, Aaron, left home to begin his studies at Savannah College of Art and Design, where he had won a ten thousand dollar scholarship competition. This left Pam and me only one child shy of being "empty nesters."

So on the morning of October 23, 1995, I reflected on our family's changes and read Chambers' question in that day's devotion with new eyes. For the first time I was able to answer, "God, this is true in my life, and I'm going to live my life in the belief that You can remove anything You desire from me without my trust in You being shaken."

Then came October 24. When the day began I had no idea that it would become the worst day of my life. The tragic date of September 11, 2001, will now be shared by many thousands of people in our country as the worst day they have ever experienced, but at least for me, October 24, 1995, remains the date "that will live in infamy."

I had traveled to Grand Rapids, Michigan, for a business meeting, when I received a phone call from my sister at home in Atlanta. I expected her to give me bad news about my mother, who had been very ill. Instead, she told me my son Aaron had just had a massive brain hemorrhage and had been taken to a hospital in Savannah for emergency brain surgery. She and my wife, Pam, were now making plans to fly there immediately.

The quickest flight I could find routed me through Milwaukee and Atlanta, then to Savannah, so I would never make it there before Aaron's surgery. But I wanted to talk to the surgeon to find out firsthand what he anticipated and to let him know I would be praying for him as well as for Aaron. Between planes in Milwaukee I called the hospital.

I take great comfort when I look back and see the sovereign hand of God at work, even in our most trying times. Aaron usually drove to his first class of the day, which met across campus. On this day, however, the class had been moved to the library, just a short walk from his dorm. He awoke that morning with a headache, but went ahead and dressed for class. Walking to the library, though, his headache worsened, and he decided he should go back to his room. Had he made it, he probably would have bled to death. Instead, the pain got so bad he sat on a bench in one of Savannah's historic parks and called out for help. He was beginning to lose his vision, and his speech became difficult because of pressure that the quickly forming blood clot was putting on his brain. Within a matter of a couple of hours, the clot had become the size of a tennis ball.

As he lay on the bench, calling out for help, a number of people walked past him. They must have thought, "Here's a kid strung out on drugs who's getting what he deserves." Like the man in the story of the Good Samaritan, Aaron was being ignored by those walking past him. If that had continued much longer, he simply would have fallen into a coma and quietly died.

A few weeks earlier Aaron had met a young lady who on this particular day was celebrating her eighteenth birthday. She had received a notice that she had a package at the post office, so she walked in a direction she normally would not have taken to get her birthday present. Along the way she saw, but at first did not recognize, Aaron lying on the park bench. When she stopped and asked what she could do to help, she realized something was terribly wrong. Asking another friend she saw to stay with Aaron, she ran to call 911.

Paramedics arrived and had no idea what was wrong with Aaron, who was almost incoherent by then. "What hospital do you want to go to?" they asked.

He tried to say, "Just take me to where the doctors are!" But the blood clot in his head was already affecting the speech part of his brain. He finally struggled to say, "Just take me to where the monsters are!" At this, I'm sure the paramedics must have thought he was on drugs as well.

"I don't know the surgeon's name," I told the operator, "but

I have to talk with him quickly. I'm about to board another plane."

I'm sure there are many operators at Memorial Medical Center, the largest hospital in Savannah, but none could have been more caring and understanding than the one who took my call.

"Sir, I know what you're going through," she said. "My son was recently in a motorcycle wreck and had surgery in this hospital. I thought he was going to die, but he pulled through. Please hang on, and I'll find out who your son's surgeon is and get him on the line if at all possible."

Every few minutes, then, she came back and said, "Are you still there? Keep hanging on. I'm determined to find him."

Finally the surgeon came on the phone. "Is Aaron going to live?" I asked immediately.

I know that in situations like that, when you're traveling from far away, they want you to be as calm as possible, so I was skeptical when he answered, "Yes, he'll live."

Then he got to the truth of the matter. The blood clot was putting nearly fatal pressure on Aaron's brain. "When you get here," he said, "Aaron will be out of surgery, on a respirator, and unable to talk. And I must tell you that he may never talk again, see again, or walk again."

These were not comforting words, but I had wanted the truth. "I want you to know," I told the surgeon, "that many people are already praying for Aaron—and for you."

He brushed my comment aside, seeming confident in his own ability. Nurses later told us Aaron's doctor was the finest brain surgeon in Savannah.

So I boarded the plane deep in thought, wondering if I would see my son alive again, remembering times of joy and sorrow, thankful for his confession of faith and his walk with the Lord. Then somewhere over Georgia between Atlanta and Savannah, I felt the Lord say to me, "Jim, did you mean what you said yesterday? Do you have such a trust in Me that you no longer seek My blessings, but only Me?"

From the day God had given Aaron to Pam and me, we knew he was a gift of God and that He had simply "loaned" Aaron to us. I prayed, "God, I absolutely meant it. If you want Aaron more than I need him, You may have him." Then I began to weep.

When I arrived at the hospital, I saw that the surgeon had been mistaken. Aaron was not on a respirator. He was able to speak, to see, and to move all his limbs. The surgery had been extremely successful. He had a tube running out of his head to drain fluid, and a big incision ran from his left ear to the top of his head where they had opened his skull with a saw. But he was alive! And my heart overflowed with joy to the Lord for sparing him.

I was glad that it was not until much later that I discovered that eighty-five percent of the people who have the type of brain hemorrhage that Aaron had die as a result.

Of the fifteen percent who live, half have a major mental or physical disability throughout their life. Aaron was indeed a miracle!

Perhaps you have experienced a similar trial with a member of your family, but God did not answer your prayers in the way you would have hoped. As I have shared Aaron's miraculous story with others, I have often thought, "What if God had chosen to take him home to be with Him?" I pray I would have responded properly, understanding that God's will is always best, regardless of the cost—and also understanding that His grace would have still been extended to me and my family and that it would not mean He loves us any less. After all—"God is good" all the time (Psalm 73:1), and He said, " 'My grace is sufficient for you, for my power is made perfect in weakness' " (2 Corinthians 12:9).

Although Aaron's life had been spared, the doctor told us that the weeks, months, and perhaps even years ahead would be difficult. Aaron could talk, but his words were completely jumbled. He had difficulty forming sentences, and he could no longer read and write. Although the computer animation skills in the "artsy" side of the brain were still intact, his ability to type had been nearly erased from his memory. In many ways he was starting over again.

But first we had to get him home. For six days he remained in intensive care while Pam and I spent as much time with him as possible. Late on the fourth night, when we were hungry—but tired of the hospital cafeteria food—

I said, "I'm going out to get us something to eat."

I didn't know anything about Savannah; I just got in the car and drove to the first open restaurant I saw, a pizza place in a small shopping center. Nobody was inside except one young man behind the counter. I went in and ordered our pizza, then waited, deep in my thoughts. After several minutes of silence the young man asked where I was from, and we struck up a conversation. I told him about Aaron, and he assured me of the fine care at the hospital.

"I was in there myself not too long ago," he said.

"Really?" I said. "What for?"

"I was in a bad motorcycle accident. Almost died."

Before I could ask him, he added, "My mother works at the hospital."

A wave of joy almost lifted me off the floor as I remembered my conversation with the hospital operator whose son had been in the hospital after a motocycle accident. I said, "Your mother helped me out on the telephone the other day. She got the surgeon for me. She was so thoughtful. I'd love to thank her."

He looked over my shoulder and said, "Well, here she comes right now."

His mother stepped in from the parking lot, and I told her who I was and how God had worked through her life to comfort and encourage me. I was so grateful for that opportunity to express my gratitude and to share how the Lord had used her to minister to me. Only God could have put that scenario together!

Aaron came home with us a couple of days later, and the hard work of recovery was about to begin: speech therapy, physical therapy, and relearning many of the basic skills of living. After we had put away all his things from school, I went to the computer to check my E-mail. While Aaron was in intensive care, Zondervan Publishing House had tried to contact me to ask if I would be interested in updating L.B. Cowman's *Streams in the Desert*. As I look back on this today, I see this timing as nothing short of miraculous. God knew I needed the words of comfort offered in *Streams in the Desert* as Aaron and our family worked through his recovery.

DIVINE PRUNING

Less than a month after we took Aaron home, my mother had to undergo a colonoscopy. Her physician had incorrectly prescribed a double dose of a medication that caused intestinal bleeding, and the blood led to concerns that she might have a tumor. The colonoscopy showed no tumor, but during the procedure the doctor perforated my mother's colon. He then performed emergency surgery to repair the perforation, but ten days later the internal stitches broke loose, causing infection, and she went back for emergency surgery. For thirty days, while Pam took Aaron back and forth to Shepherd Spinal Center in

Atlanta for therapy, I took turns with my sisters staying with Mother at the hospital as she recovered.

A month later, Pam and our youngest child, Bethany, were traveling on an Atlanta interstate highway when their car was rear-ended. I began to wonder how much more we could take. They both suffered whiplash and had to go to the doctor almost daily for a few weeks.

That same December my hands began to hurt as I worked on the updated edition of *Streams in the Desert*. It would be 2001 before I realized this was the onset of carpal tunnel syndrome (something I finally had repaired with surgery just weeks before writing this book), but back in late 1995 and early 1996 I had just about had it with whatever God was doing with us. "God," I prayed, "You've called me to be a writer, and now You're allowing my hands to be afflicted with this pain. What good am I going to be to You if I can't type?"

I vividly remember going into my quiet time one morning a few weeks later and praying, "God, I'm obviously not understanding whatever it is You're trying to teach me here. Either I'm too stupid or too slow to learn, because You apparently think You have to keep allowing all these difficulties in my life.

"Why don't You just take these problems and visit them on somebody else—not that I would wish them on my worst enemy—because I must not be understanding Your message for me, and I apparently am not going to understand it. I think You should just give up on me and quit sending these problems our way."

Upon ending my quiet time—such as it was—I went into my office to begin another day writing the new edition of *Streams in the Desert*. The work had turned out to be all I had hoped, ministering to me with the hope, encouragement, comfort, and strength of God's word. But nothing had prepared me for what appeared on my screen following my "little talk" with God.

The devotion I worked on that day was the reading for February 19, and the Scripture that accompanied it was John 15:2, "Every branch that does bear fruit he prunes so that it will be even more fruitful."

Then L. B. Cowman quoted these words from Homera Homer-Dixon:

A child of God was once overwhelmed by the number of afflictions that seemed to target her. As she walked past a vineyard during the rich glow of autumn, she noticed its untrimmed appearance and the abundance of leaves still on the vines. The ground had been overtaken by a tangle of weeds and grass, and the entire place appeared totally unkempt. While she pondered the sight, the heavenly Gardener whispered such a precious message to her that she could not help but share it.

The message was this: "My dear child, are you questioning the number of trials in your life?

> *Remember the vineyard and learn from it. The gar-*
> *dener stops pruning and trimming the vine or weed-*
> *ing the soil only when he expects nothing more from*
> *the vine during that season. He leaves it alone,*
> *because its fruitfulness is gone and further effort now*
> *would yield no profit. In the same way, freedom from*
> *suffering leads to uselessness. Do you now want me*
> *to stop pruning your life? Shall I leave you alone?"*
>
> *Then her comforted heart cried, "No!"*

I had told the Lord, "No more," but He knew exactly what I needed. He saw fruit that I didn't see, so he pruned me and my family.

We experience wave after wave of difficulty, even failure, despite our earnest prayers to God, and we wonder aloud, "Lord, do You ever listen to me?"

The Lord had spoken to me clearly. He was pruning me, shaping me, molding me, using these experiences to conform me to the image of His Son—to produce in me fruit I could not see. He had not given me anything I could not bear, and He promised that He would not do so.

He had reminded me that freedom from suffering leads to uselessness. We get spiritually lazy, spiritually "fat, dumb, and happy," when we are not pruned through suffering.

The apostle Paul chose to endure a second kind of suffering for Christ's sake. He preached boldly when he knew his words would lead to his flogging, imprisonment, or death.

But Paul said he was happy to suffer for Christ's sake because that suffering established him as one to share in an eternal inheritance. He goes so far as to use legal language to assert his place, and ours, in the family of God. "Now if we are children, then we are heirs—heirs of God and co-heirs with Christ, if indeed we share in his sufferings in order that we may also share in his glory" (Romans 8:17).

God calls us His children, because, from a purely legal standpoint, children do something that flows naturally from being in that position: they inherit! Yet the Lord clearly states that if we expect to "share in His glory," we must indeed "share in His sufferings."

We in America have never experienced the persecution Paul faced. The question we must ask ourselves is, "Would we allow ourselves to be beaten, imprisoned, or killed for Christ's sake?" Or, like Oswald Chambers, are we willing to ask ourselves: "Have I come to the point where God can withdraw His blessings from me without my trust in Him being affected?"

I consider that our present sufferings
are not worth comparing with
the glory that will be revealed in us.

—ROMANS 8:18

Whatever happens,
conduct yourselves in a manner worthy of the
gospel of Christ.
Then. . .I will know that you stand firm
in one spirit, contending as one man for
the faith of the gospel without being frightened
in any way by those who oppose you.
This is a sign to them that
they will be destroyed,
but that you will be saved—and that by God.
For it has been granted to you
on behalf of Christ not only to believe on him,
but also to suffer for him.

—PHILIPPIANS 1:27–29

When Hate Gives Way to Love

You have heard that it was said,
"Love your neighbor and hate your enemy."
But I tell you: Love your enemies
and pray for those who persecute you.
—MATTHEW 5:43–44

For once, let's have no "grief counselors"
standing by with banal consolations. . . .
America needs to relearn a lost discipline. . .
called hatred.
—*TIME* MAGAZINE,
SPECIAL EDITION, SEPTEMBER 2001

Jesus seems to be asking the impossible here. Saul of Tarsus, a worldly man, would have laughed at the idea of loving his enemies, the Christians. Few Christian leaders today have been so radical as to suggest that we should love the Muslim extremists who would annihilate us, but after he was transformed, the apostle Paul not only loved his enemies, he said, "I could wish that I myself were cursed and cut off from Christ for the sake of my brothers, those of my own race, the people of Israel" (Romans 9:3–4). Paul's love for the Jews—the people who were now persecuting him and other Christians—was so great that he would have chosen eternal damnation for himself in order that they might be brought into a relationship with Christ.

All Christians, Paul says, will experience a transformation as dramatic as his own: "If anyone is in Christ, he is a new creation; the old has gone, the new has come!" (2 Corinthians 5:17).

I found my seat on the airplane and looked around. Every seat was filled except the one beside me. What a break! Finally I was going to have a few quiet moments. It had already been a long day, and I prayed that God might give me some time alone with Him on the late-afternoon flight.

The flight attendants closed the doors, and it appeared my prayer had been answered. Then a male flight attendant walked down the aisle and stopped at my row. He introduced himself to me before filling the empty seat. He was off duty and traveling to Chicago to begin his workday.

In spite of the fact that I was leaning back with my eyes closed in an obvious attempt to say, "Leave me alone," the flight attendant asked, "What do you do?"

"Write," I said, hoping my monosyllabic reply would reinforce my desire not to talk. It didn't.

"What do you write?" he asked.

"Books."

"What kind of books?"

Desiring some peace and quiet, I intentionally avoided saying, "Christian books." I simply responded, "Daily-reading books."

All I wanted was a little quiet time, and the man would not leave me alone. The last thing I wanted that day was a theological discussion with a stranger, which I knew would begin as soon as I disclosed my profession. He continued to press for details, and I finally told him, "I update Christian daily devotional books."

He turned to face me directly before saying, "I hate Christians!"

I must admit I was a little taken back by this. I had never heard anyone respond so strongly, angrily, and unashamedly to the term "Christian" before. My initial inclination was to respond in kind, but I bit my tongue and quietly asked, "Tell me why."

"I'm a homosexual," he began, "and Christians are always telling me how to live. They're always condemning me and my lifestyle. They hate me—so I just hate 'em right back!"

He didn't stop there. For at least ten minutes I sat silently while he vented his anger at me—the Christian sitting closest to him—and all the while I prayed, "God, let me hear this man's heart before I share, then open a door for your message that I 'may proclaim the mystery of Christ. . .clearly, as I should' (Colossians 4:3–4), and speak 'the truth in love' " (Ephesians 4:15).

Several times I was tempted to interrupt the man, but I kept my mouth shut while he unloaded with both barrels. The more he vented, the sadder I became—sad that he was holding such hostility and sad that he had not seen the love of Jesus in the Christians he had met.

When he finished speaking I said, "A true Christian with an intimate relationship with Jesus would not condemn you. My role as a Christian is not to condemn you or to convict you of any sin in your life. God is fully capable of that. My job is simply to tell you what has taken place in my life and to speak the truth in love. Now, I can share a lot of Scripture that means a lot to me, and you can choose to believe it or not."

"I choose not to believe the Bible," he interrupted.

"Or we could argue tenets of the faith all day long," I said, "but I don't really want to do that. But here's one thing I know: I believe Jesus Christ came to earth as the Son of God to die for my sins. There came a time in my life when I was twenty years old, and I had to come to the end of myself. I realized I needed a savior. As soon as I invited Him into my heart, I experienced a total transformation. It was amazing! I was headed one direction, and He turned me around 180 degrees, and I have never looked back. In the nearly thirty years since that day, I have experienced joy and peace that are unspeakable."

He let me continue without interruption. "I want you to know that I did not have fulfillment in my life. I lived a lifestyle different from what gospel proclaims, and I didn't have joy and peace in my life. I do now. And I'm convinced through all my searching, all the roads I took, the only way to know that joy and peace is through Jesus Christ. The only way to abundant life is through Him."

About that time the airplane landed, and I felt something like the farmer in the parable of the sower, except that the soil I had been working for over an hour was harder than the concrete runway underneath us. I knew that man didn't have joy in his life; if he had, he would not have lashed out against me as he did. And he all but told me that he had not experienced peace—not the true peace that people in this world are starving for.

We Christians don't offer peace when we tell people they're going to burn in hell if they don't stop sinning. What's the point of simply escaping hell if you spend the rest of your life as an escapee on the run? That's no way to live. Jesus said, "I am come that they might have life, and that they might have it more abundantly" (John 10:10 KJV). I want to share what Christ has done for me in my life now—this earthly life. And I have this bonus of eternal life.

Everyone around stood up to leave the plane, and the man beside me said, "Could you write down the titles of the books you've written?" I did, then he stood to walk off. Before walking away, however, he extended his right hand to me and said, "In all my years this is the only civil conversation I've ever had with a Christian."

I have no idea what happened next to him. It's apparently not for me to know in this life. But I do know that the Holy Spirit flowed through me that day, and the Lord made a crack in the concrete of that man's heart. " 'He who believes in Me. . .out of his heart will flow rivers of living water' " (John 7:38 NKJV). You may be the next person to sit beside him on an airplane. Will you turn your back to him as I almost did? Will you show him the face of hatred as he said so many other Christians have done? Or will you tell him your story and work his soil with a little more love, so that when the seed of the Holy Spirit lands in his heart, it can take root and flourish?

I encourage Christians to take every opportunity to share their testimony in a way that defies argument. You don't have to know the Bible, chapter and verse in depth, to tell your own story. You don't have to understand every theological tenet of the faith. In fact, you can't fully understand

Christ *until* you share your faith. "I pray that you may be active in sharing your faith, so that you will have a full understanding of every good thing we have in Christ" (Philemon 6). God makes something known to us in the process of sharing our faith.

Simply take the essence of the gospel "Jesus Christ and him crucified" (1 Corinthians 2:2) and tell what it has meant to you. The outline of your story is this simple: This is who I was, this is Who I met, and this is who I am today.

There's a real freedom in witnessing this way. I don't have to be condemning or proud. I have only to remember what I was. As Oswald Chambers wrote, "I've never met a man I can despair of (or lose all hope for) after discerning what lies in me apart from the grace of God."

Some might say, "But you're being too intolerant of others' beliefs and insensitive by sharing your faith so boldly at a time like this." But the answer can never be to ignore our differences as though they do not exist or to stand arm-in-arm with those who believe error, simply for the sake of so-called unity. In fact, the exact opposite is true. We show our true love and concern for others by sharing our faith! Paul wrote, "We loved you so much that we were delighted to share with you not only the gospel of God but our lives as well" (1 Thessalonians 2:8).

It isn't complicated. You don't need any special training. Just tell your story, exhibit Jesus Christ crucified, and lift Him up in your life for all to see. When you do, many will understand his words, " 'My command is this: Love each other as I have loved you. Greater love has no one than this, that he lay down his life for his friends. You are my friends if you do what I command' " (John 15:12–14).

THE REST OF YOUR LIFE

On September 11, 2001, we saw the true meaning of Christ's words as people ran into the World Trade Center towers and the Pentagon to save the lives of others. Ten days later I attended a benefit dinner in Atlanta supporting the Christian Embassy, a Washington, D.C., ministry that reaches out to elected officials, political appointees, and anyone else involved in the government or the military. The speaker, U.S. Navy Captain Tom Joyce, put away his previously prepared remarks.

Captain Joyce's office was on the fifth floor of the Pentagon, directly above the impact point of the hijacked airliner that was deliberately flown into the building. Standing near his desk, he was knocked five feet across the floor, but he and his staff of seventy people were able to get out safely before their offices were totally engulfed in flames and collapsed. Captain Joyce then joined the rescue effort.

Several minutes earlier a colleague of Captain Joyce's in Navy Intelligence, Lieutenant Commander Chuck Capets, had called to report the first attack in New York. Capets called again following the second New York attack, and as they discussed the situation Commander Capets literally saw the nose of the airplane smash into the Pentagon just to the right of where he was standing. In the instant devastation he saw a hole in the wall near the nose of the plane, and he headed toward the light. Once outside he realized nobody had followed him out, so he ran back into the fire that had erupted behind him and dragged two people to safety.

When Captain Joyce asked him why he had gone back in, he responded, "That's what we're trained to do. First, we save our shipmates. Second, we save our ship. Third, we save ourselves. So I went in."

Commander Capets had indeed been willing to " 'lay down his life for his friends' " (John 15:13). Captain Joyce related Capets' unselfish actions to that of Jesus who " 'did not come to be served, but to serve, and to give his life as a ransom for many' " (Matthew 20:28).

When he had done all he could do at the Pentagon on September 11, Captain Joyce drove home, where his wife and children ran out the front door to greet him. They hugged, then stood in the front yard and prayed. When the "amens" were said, his seventeen-year-old son said, "So, Dad, what are you going to do with the rest of your life?"

That's the real question, isn't it? Despite deaths in conflicts across the world or on highways and in hospitals around the globe this very day, you and I have been blessed with another day to live.

What are you going to do with today? Will you stand up and say, "In God I trust," then live your life as if you mean it?

Not only have you been rescued to live another day, you can be rescued to eternal life. Like the firefighters and policemen in New York City, like the rescuers at the Pentagon, Jesus Christ came to earth and laid down His life for you and me, not because He loves America or any other country—for, "While we were still sinners, Christ died for us" (Romans 5:8)—but because He loves every person who ever lived and every person alive today. He carries us on His shoulders into eternity when we say, "Take me, Lord."

Then He says to us:

Follow Me!

The man who loves his life will lose it,
while the man who hates his life
in this world will keep it for eternal life.
Whoever serves me must follow me;
and where I am, my servant also will be.
My Father will honor the one who serves me.

—JOHN 12:25–26

All men will hate you because of me.
But not a hair of your head will perish.
By standing firm you will gain life. . .
Everyone born of God overcomes the world.
This is the victory that has overcome the world,
even our faith.
Who is it that overcomes the world?
Only he who believes that
Jesus is the Son of God.
—LUKE 21:17–19, 1 JOHN 5:4–5

About the Author

Jim Reimann is editor of the highly acclaimed, updated editions of *My Utmost for His Highest* and *Streams in the Desert*, both longtime best-sellers. Most recently he edited the updated version of Victor Hugo's classic *Les Misérables*. He formerly owned and operated a very successful bookstore called the Christian Armory in Atlanta, Georgia, and has served as chairman of the board of the Christian Booksellers Association. Reimann and his wife, Pam, now own Streams Tours, a ministry offering teaching tours of Israel (www.streamstours.com).